Dedication:

Thank you to God

Thank you to my husband Paul and our wonderful children;
Dallas, Hunter, Chandler, Austin, Gavin & Savanna

Thank you to my mother & father for believing in a dreamer

Thank you to my awesome friends and family on Facebook for your inspiration.

And a special thank you to Mrs. Jenny Matteson for all of her technical support and computer knowledge, you are truly an amazing woman.

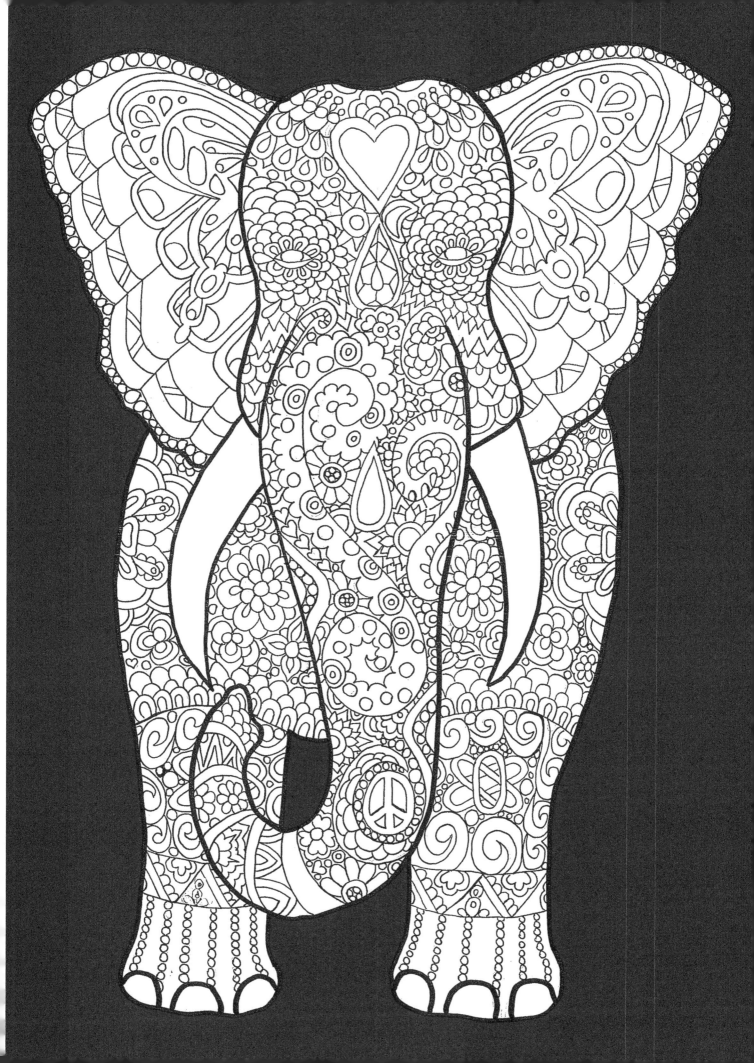

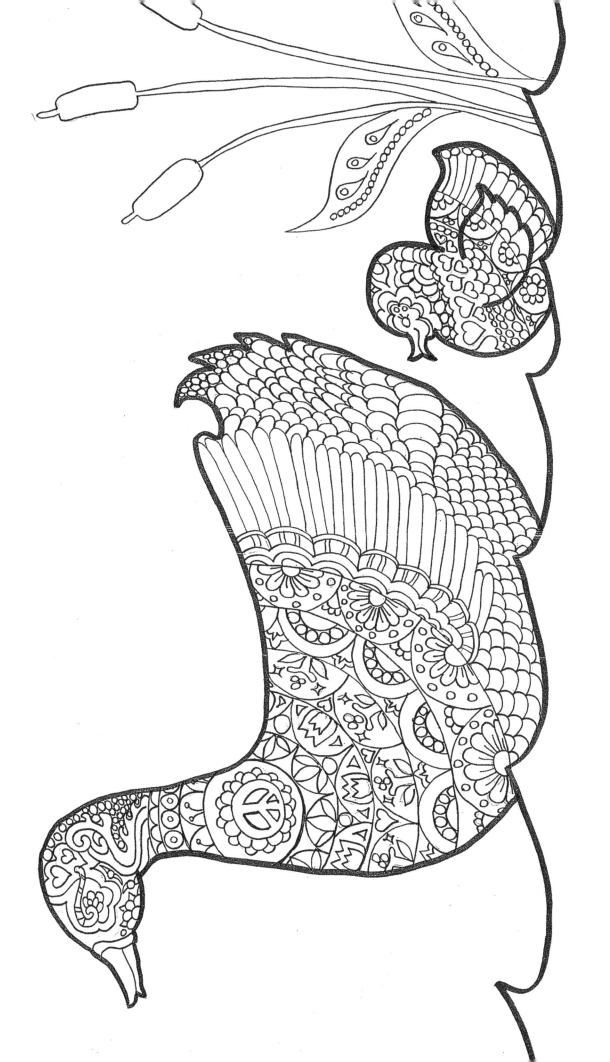

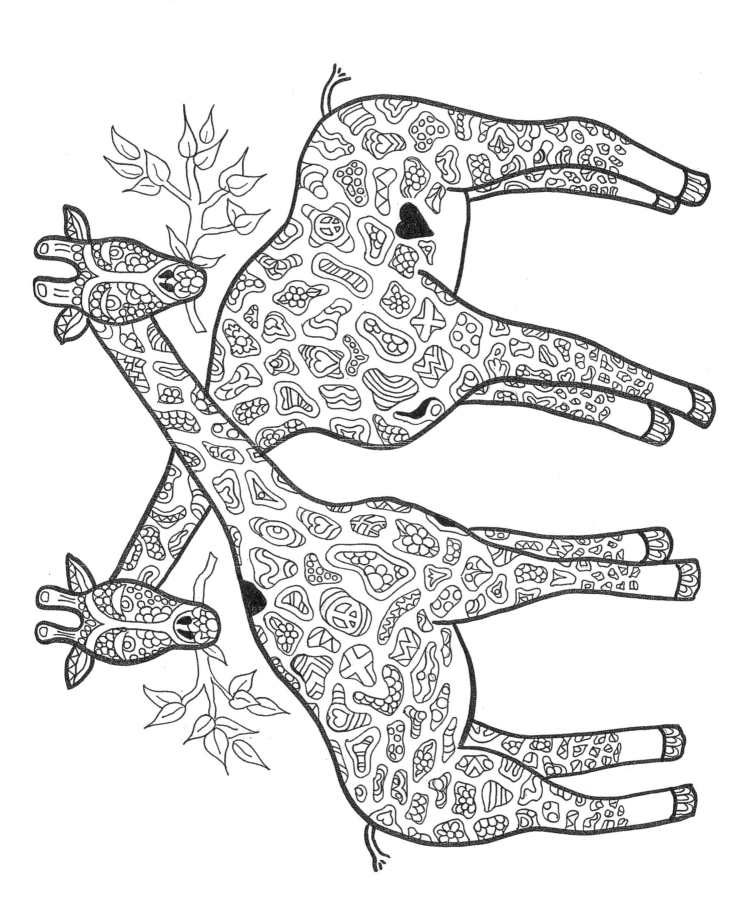

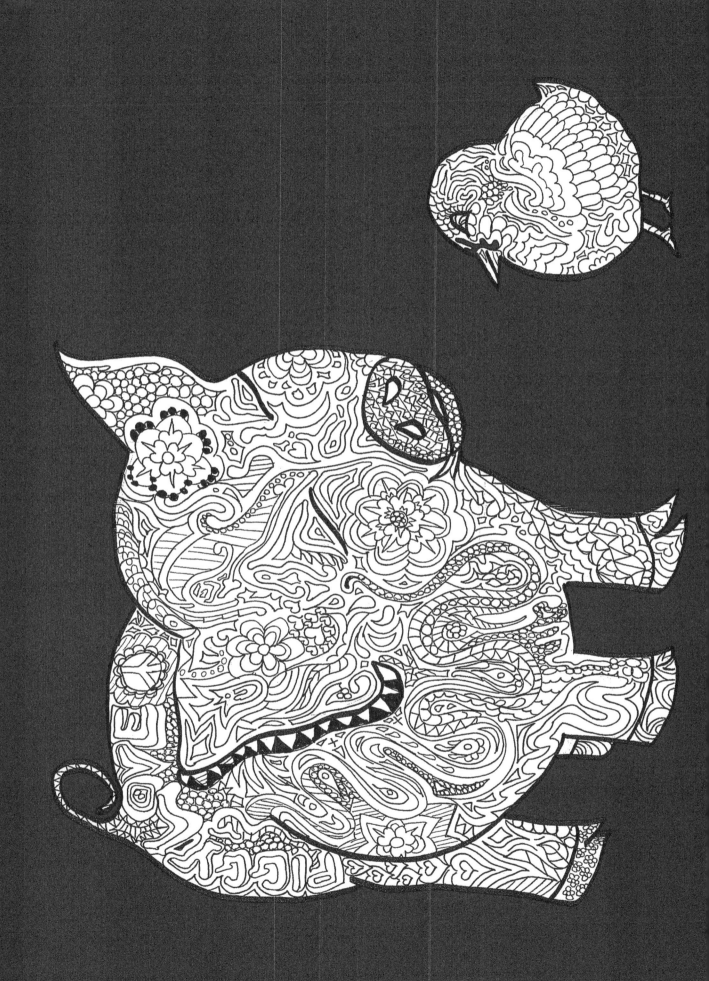

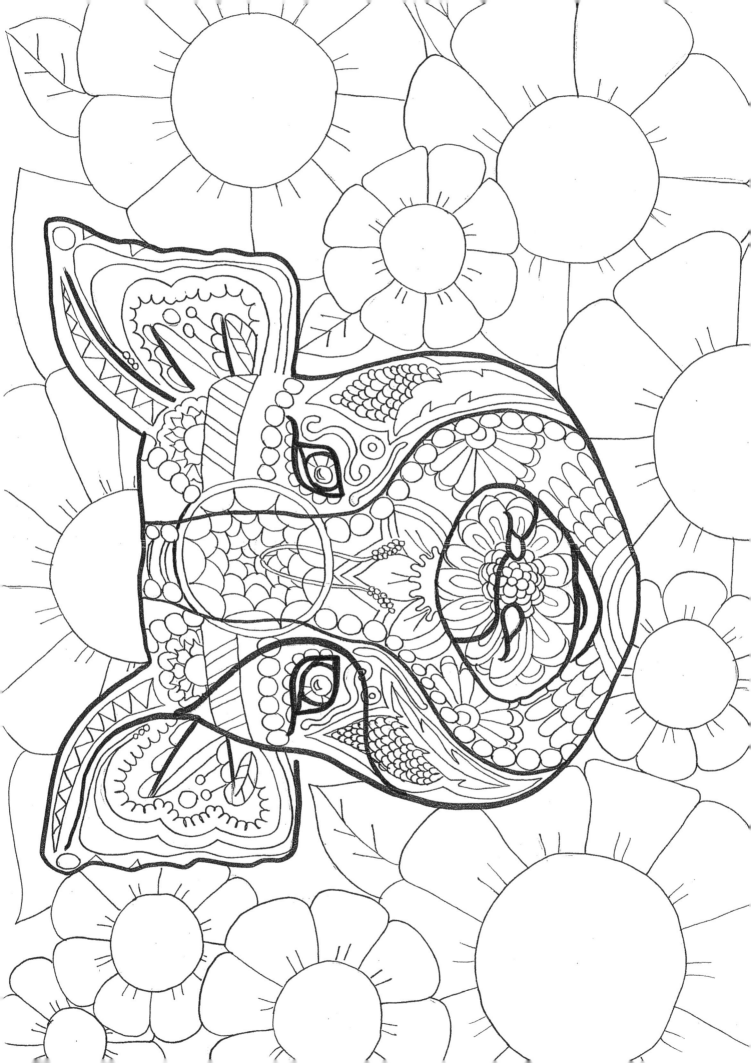

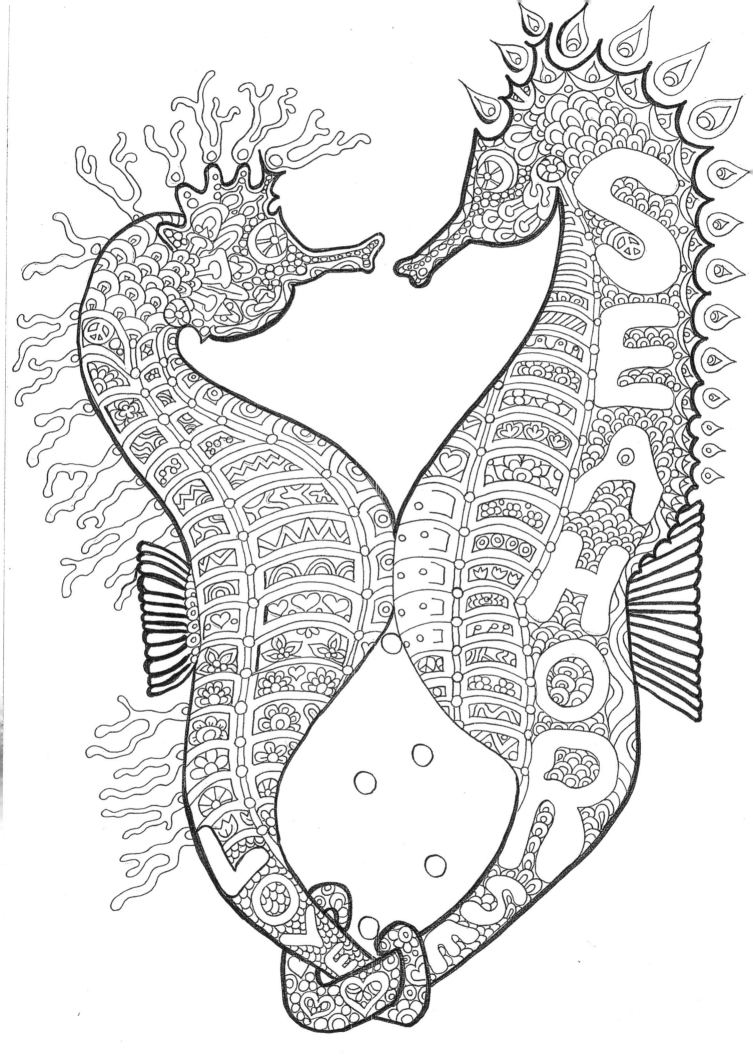

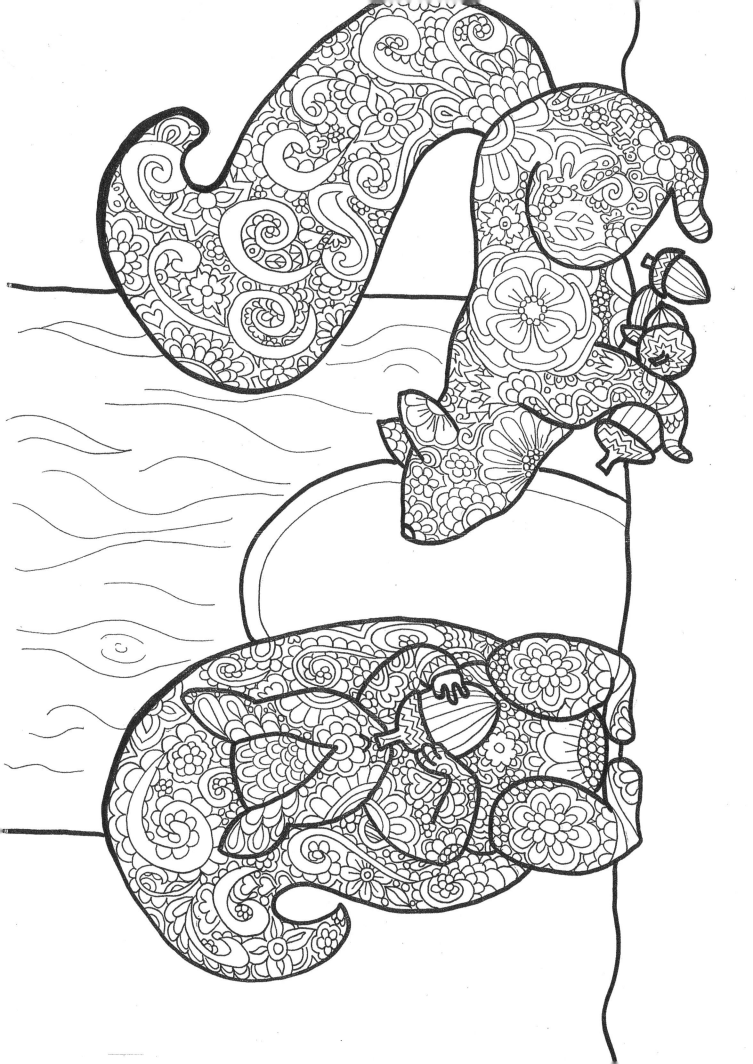

Made in the USA
Columbia, SC
24 January 2022